unto us

AN ADVENT DEVOTIONAL

by Jessica Broberg

All Scripture quotations, unless otherwise indicated, are taken from THE MESSAGE. Copyright 1993, 1994, 1995, 1996, 2000, 2001, 2002. Used by permission of NavPress Publishing Group.

Oh, Come, All Ye Faithful. Text: Attr. to John F. Wade, ca. 1711-1786; trans. by Frederick Oakeley, 1802-1880. Music: Attr. to John F. Wade.

Better Homes and Gardens. Holiday Biscotti. Retrieved from www.bhg.com

My Recipes.com Christmas with Southern Living. 2004. Mesclun Salad with Cranberries and Avocado. Retrieved from www.myrecipes.com

Edited by: Crystal Stine
Water Color Art by: Elsa McPherson
Book Design by: Dena Swenson

ISBN: 978-0-578-19734-0

Printed in United States of America

1st Printing

# Acknowledgement

Aaron, words can't explain how much I love and appreciate you. You have been my very best friend for the last 17 years, and you continue to show me in very tangible ways what it means to put that love into action. Without you, this book wouldn't be a reality. You believed in me even when I was unsure of myself. You are the very best gift God has ever given me! Thank you for all the time you spent researching information and helping me through this process. But even more than your time and your tech-savvy talent, thank you for your enthusiasm. It's contagious, and it kept me going more times than I can count. Love you.

To my kiddos: Jacob, Levi & Hannah. I love you guys more than you can know. Thank you for allowing me time to write. Thank you for understanding that writing is just part of who your mom is. I pray I can model for you what it looks like to be someone who balances all that they've been entrusted. Because even though I've been called to write, my greatest calling will always be being your mom.

To my parents: I owe so much of who I am to you. I love you both with all of my heart and I am so incredibly grateful for the spiritual blessings you have passed on to me.

To my siblings: Meredith, Josh & Gabe. Writing this devotional has taken me back to our childhood. We have made so many wonderful memories over the years. I am so thankful for each of you and the unique ways you have helped shape my life.

To Angie who made me believe I was a writer, to Israel who shared this dream with me and to Sarah to who has championed every word I have ever written, you girls have been such a blessing to me in this process. Thank you for all the love and encouragement over the years.

# Contents

# Introduction

Dear friend,

I am so excited to start this advent season with you! What a perfect time it is to realign our hearts and focus on the birth of our Savior, Jesus. Unto us. These two words found in Isaiah chapter 9 are a prophetic declaration of all that was ahead for mankind. "*Unto us a child is born, unto us a son is given.*" (Isaiah 9:6, KJV) And because of this, we have been offered even so much more in Christ. Unto us is forgiveness of sins, salvation, hope for our future, peace that sustains us in the midst of our trials and a friendship with the God of the universe.

We have been given so much!

I pray that over these next few weeks, as we take time to look at some of the wonderful gifts that have been made available to us through Jesus Christ, our lives would be altered by the grace He has for us. I pray that we would rediscover the true joy, lasting hope and steadfast peace that is only found in Him.

As you make your way through the book, you will find three weeks of devotionals. It may be helpful to know that Monday - Friday will be a written devotional, with Saturday and Sunday focused on a time of rest and reflection that includes art, Scripture and some of my favorite recipes.

It is an honor that you would allow me to share a part of myself with you. I have prayed over these words and believe with all my heart that the Holy Spirit will take them and shape them in a personal way to speak to each heart individually. He knows our needs, sees our hearts and can reach us in deeply personal ways.

> *Father, we invite you into our hearts and lives. We pray that you would take these moments, these words, and your truth to reveal to our hearts what you want to speak to us. I pray that during this holiday season we would receive all that you have for us. Give us eyes to see the beauty, the broken, and the needy. We place it all in your hands Father, trusting you to work it together for your glory and our good. Amen.*

Much love,
Jess

"FOR A CHILD
HAS BEEN BORN—FOR US!

THE GIFT
OF A SON—FOR US!"

ISAIAH 9:6
(THE MESSAGE)

# Unto Us

These two small words introduce us to God's plan for mankind's redemption story. Though they are small in length, they stand tall in meaning and shout wildly with joy, declaring the coming of our King. Unto you. Unto me. Unto us.

> *"For a child has been born – for us!*
> *the gift of a son – for us!"* Isaiah 9:6 (The Message)

**A Wonderful Counselor for us.**

**A Mighty God for us.**

**An Everlasting Father for us.**

**A Prince of Peace for us.**

Every title, name, and promise, wrapped up in one tiny package and gently placed in a feeding trough. Our redemption waits for us in a manger.

Amidst a season of rushing and scrambling to find that perfect gift for a loved one, we are reminded again that the greatest gift anyone could ever possibly receive has already been given. The gift of our Savior in the form of a baby. Just like bringing home a newborn causes us to slow down, to take a break from our frantic pace and embrace the miracle of new life, this advent season also invites us to halt our hectic lives and take a moment to simply embrace Jesus.

Let the gift of who He is settle over you today. The Mighty God came for you. His plan included you because his heart is for you. Whether you've already accepted this gift or you're just beginning to unwrap the depth of His love for you, salvation and rest are available to you today in Christ.

During this Advent season, we will be taking some time to look at the amazing promises that have been given unto us through Jesus. From His royal titles to His faithful promises, each of a prized possession passed down to us from a loving Father. Let's prepare our hearts and wait on Him as we look forward with anticipation to the celebration of Christmas and the gift of God's one and only Son, Jesus.

> *"For unto us a child is born; unto us a son is given; and the government shall be upon his shoulders. These will be his royal titles: "Wonderful," "Counselor, "The Mighty God," "The Everlasting Father, " "The Prince of Peace." His ever expanding peaceful government will never end. He will rule with perfect fairness and justice from the throne of his father David. He will bring true justice and peace to all the nations of the world. This is going to happen because the Lord of heaven's armies has dedicated himself to do it!"* Isaiah 9:6-7 (TLB)

# Good Gifts

I still remember the Christmas when I received one of my favorite gifts ever as a child.

We had just finished opening presents and my brothers and sister and I were on clean up detail. First, we set to work gathering all our treasures into individual piles. All discarded plastic packaging went into a giant black garbage bag, but all gift bags, ribbons, and bows (sometimes even wrapping paper if it was in decent shape) was salvaged for use again the following year. There were years when I would retrieve a gift from under the tree and spend the next several minutes trying to decipher whose it was. Usually, three or four different names had been written down in various ink colors and then crossed off. My mom got a lot of mileage out of her gift bags. Oddly enough, I married into a family that does this same thing.

We were almost done cleaning when my dad nonchalantly mentioned that Santa brought one more gift for me and it was waiting in the basement. I bolted down the stairs to discover my very own kitchen play set, complete with a sink, microwave, refrigerator, and oven. To this day I can remember the excitement I felt realizing my parents had given me the perfect gift.

Countless hours were spent downstairs, pretending to whip up delicious food, wash the dishes, and stock the fridge after grocery shopping. In fact, that kitchen set moved outside for an entire summer the year my siblings and I acted out the Boxcar Children books. Those were the days when parents would shove their children out the door in the morning and expect them to entertain themselves. There was usually the opportunity for re-entry sometime around noon for lunch, and then again at supper time. But for the most part, we spent that summer entertaining ourselves and pretending to live in a boxcar. I have so many wonderful memories connected to that play kitchen.

That Christmas I was given a great gift.

One of the greatest things about a good gift is that it's given willingly and nothing is expected in return. My parents knew I was going to love that play kitchen and they wanted to give it to me without any payment on my part. There was nothing that I had to do on my end other than to accept it. Their desire was to give me a good gift simply because they loved me.

God does the same, only better.

He extends gifts like salvation, patience, peace, joy, wisdom, and comfort. He gives remarkable gifts to us because of His great love **for us**. We need only accept them.

Today may we remember that although earthly gifts are good and can even hold wonderful memories for us, there is nothing that comes close to the gift of Jesus.

> *Thank you, God that you extend Your gift of salvation to us with no strings attached. Thank you that we don't have to wonder whether the gift is for us. Your gift of salvation is clearly marked for each of us. You desire to give us good gifts simply because You love us. Thank you again for Your perfect gifts.*

# A Child is Born

Is there anything more exciting than the news of a baby being born?

As I am typing this, my sister-in-law is in labor. She's having baby number three today. I have checked my phone every five minutes for the last hour just waiting for the call or text to announce her arrival. Although the days leading up to the delivery have been long and hard for her (chasing a three-year-old and one-and-a-half-year-old around the house while maneuvering a protruding belly and holding down a full-time job), I know that the minute baby arrives she will gaze into that sweet face and everything else will melt away.

Why? Because babies are a celebration of life, love, and new beginnings. They signal a new chapter about to be written in the family's story. They usher in a sense of awe, gratefulness, and hope. Babies are the culmination of creation, pointing us back to our ultimate Creator. There is something so perfect about a newborn. New life has a way of rallying us all together to celebrate, connecting our hearts and our lives in a powerfully unique way.

And so it was for the shepherds who found their way to baby Jesus all those years ago. The setting looked a bit different than our modern-day hospital rooms and birthing centers, but the palpable excitement that settled over that stable was undeniable. THIS **good news**, THIS **new life**, was not just for a few gathered around the manger, but was instead for all mankind, for all eternity. It was for you. For me. For every person that is yet to be.

Baby Jesus was the good news that would bring great joy for all the people! This baby wrapped up in swaddling clothes would usher in a thrill of hope like nothing the world had ever seen or heard before. I can't help but believe that the shepherds, as they shared in the celebration, began to feel something give way: in their hearts, in their lives, in the very air that they were breathing. An expectancy, an anticipation, a feeling that somehow

13

this was what they had been waiting for their entire lives. A feeling that something was about to shift and, with it, the potential to change not only their lives but also the lives of every generation to come. Our salvation, wrapped in swaddling clothes and lying in a manger.

*Father, pervade our hearts with the same expectancy that the shepherds felt all those years ago. Fill us with a thrill of hope for all that You are and all that You yet have planned for us. Today we believe again for the dreams You have placed inside of us. God, help us learn to trust Your heart and to trust Your timing. Thank you Father, that You were then and you are still, our good news.*

# Hope for Right Now

John 3:16

It is probably the most well-known Bible verse of all time. *"For God so loved the world that he gave his one and only Son, that whoever believes in Him shall not perish but have eternal life."* (NIV) The Message paraphrase says this, *"This is how much God loved the world: He gave his Son, his one and only Son. And this is why: so that no one need be destroyed; by believing in him, anyone can have a whole and lasting life."*

I love this verse. I do. It's the introduction to God's love story for us all. It reveals God's character and His plan. It's inclusive, and teeming with love. But it's the following verse, John 3:17, that reads like an exclamation point to me. *"God didn't go to all the trouble of sending his Son merely to point an accusing finger, telling the world how bad it was. He came to help, to put the world right again."* (MSG)

So many people go through life believing that God goes around pointing an accusing finger, shaking His head in disappointment and sighing at our shortcomings and failures. But it's simply not true. His heart is to help, not to condemn. He sent His only Son into the world to set it right again....to set us right again.

He is our hope. **Not just for life everlasting, but for life right now.**

God's hope is available to us whether we're drowning in a sea of laundry or a sea of depression. We can experience true joy whether life seems relatively easy or we are walking through some of our darkest days. We can learn to trust His heart whether our circumstances make sense or not. We have hope for this life right now because Jesus didn't just come to tell us how bad things are, but He came to help make things better.

Whether this season finds you thriving or just barely surviving, the truth remains the same. God is our hope and He came to mend things.

*Thank you, Father, that You alone are our hope. Whether we feel especially hopeful or not, You remain our constant. Help us truly believe that You are not in a continual state of disappointment with us, but rather that You delight in us. Psalm 149 reminds us that You delight in Your people and You crown the humble with victory. Father today, crown us with Your victory. As we humble ourselves before You, please mend broken hearts and fractured relationships. Thank you for coming to help. We look forward to the day when all will be set right by You forever.*

a
thrill
of
hope

# A Son is Given

Firstborns are special.

I say that not because I am a firstborn but because of how I felt when I held my first child.

I remember that nervous yet exhilarating feeling of having his tiny little body placed into my arms for the very first time. He was **_wrapped up tight_** in a blanket and I was **_undone_**. The depth of my love for him was so intense and so immediate; it took me by surprise. Suddenly, and almost without warning, I realized I would do anything for this child of mine. Not only had I given birth, but something had been birthed inside of me. A desire to love and protect this little life at any cost.

I imagine that Mary felt the same way. Although she didn't have an adjustable bed and big fluffy pillows behind her as she drank in the first few hours of her son's life, I can imagine she felt those same feelings of intense love and fierce devotion.

Parental love—and fear—is an authentic and tangible universal language.

I can't help but wonder how Mary managed those fears as she watched her little boy mature into a young man. I wonder if she lost sleep worrying about him and his future. I wonder if she ever felt not enough at times, questioning whether she was equipped for the monumental task of motherhood. All of her time, energy and love poured out into this life that would ultimately lay itself down for us all.

**The precious gift she had been given would eventually be a gift for all mankind.** A gift of love, quite literally, as 1 John tells us that "God is love."

In our earthly understanding of love, one of our best representations is that between mother and child. It is a bond so strong that it gives us a small glimpse into the **immeasurable depth of love that God has for each of us**. Paul tells us in Ephesians 3 that he prays that

19

we will have the power to understand the greatness of Christ's love—how wide, how long, how high, and how deep that love is.

We serve a God who gives us small daily reminders of that love. From a child's laugh to the warmth of a loved one's hand, these are reflections of His love for us. As we gather this holiday season with family and friends may we sense, more deeply, the greatness of Christ's love for us. May we catch another glimpse of the height and the depth of His love and may it secure within us a sense of trust so we can walk in confidence of the love He has, not only for us, but also for the world.

*Father, we thank You today for the gift of Your Son. We thank You for the blessings You have given us in the form of our children. Father, continue to teach us more about Your love. Help us to walk in the love You have for us, and help us give that same love to those around us. We acknowledge that our confidence comes from being secure in the immeasurable love You have for each of us.*

# Rest + Recipe

## EGG NOG + HOLIDAY BISCOTTI

The holidays are the perfect time to pull out those old tried and true family recipes. When I married into the Broberg family, I quickly discovered that they had a lot of family favorites. Among a mound of delicious recipes, the one for their homemade Egg Nog stands above them all. I have made this recipe too many times to count, and every time I make it, I get the same response: "This is delicious!" I have had devout non-egg nog drinkers sing its praises. It's that good. I inevitably get asked for the recipe and whether or not it's hard to make. The answer is no; it's not hard. There are a few steps to it, but the finished product is worth every blessed calorie you will consume. Plus, it's the holidays, calories don't count, right?

## EGG NOG

### INGREDIENTS:

- *1 dozen egg yolks (beaten)*
- *1 c. sugar*
- *1 pt. half and half*
- *1 c. heavy whipping cream*
- *1 qt. egg nog*

- *1 gallon whole milk*
- *vanilla to taste*
- *rum flavoring to taste*
- *nutmeg to garnish*
- *yield ~ 1 ½ gallons*

### DIRECTIONS:

1. Separate the egg yolks.
2. Beat the egg yolks with the sugar.
3. Whip the heavy whipping cream until stiff peaks form.

4. Mix all cold ingredients together. (You will need a very large bowl or container to do this in.)

5. Add the spices to taste. I love vanilla, so I usually go a little heavy on that. We use imitation rum flavoring but if rum is your thing, then, by all means, go for it. A little nutmeg on top is the perfect garnish. And if you have mint, a small mint leaf in each mug is the perfect color complement. I dare you to drink just one glass. Enjoy!

The perfect pairing to your Egg Nog is this Holiday Biscotti recipe. This recipe has a few steps to it as well, but it makes a nice large batch, so you don't have to worry about making it too many times. Well, that may not be entirely true. I have been known to hide a half batch or so of these so the kids (and the husband) don't devour them too quickly. I found this recipe several years ago, and it has quickly become a favorite. It has made its way into the elite rank of "Christmas cookie must-haves" for our family, and if you make it, you'll see why.

# HOLIDAY BISCOTTI

## INGREDIENTS:

- *1/4 c. butter, softened*
- *1 c. sugar*
- *1 t. baking powder*
- *1/2 t. baking soda*
- *1/4 t. salt*
- *3 eggs*
- *1/2 t. vanilla*
- *1/4 t. almond extract*

- *2 1/4 c. flour*
- *1 1/2 t. anise seed*
- *1/2 t. fennel seed*
- *1 c. dried cranberries*
- *1/2 c. dried apricots*
- *3/4 c. pistachios, shelled*
- *1 egg*
- *White chocolate chips or almond bark*

## DIRECTIONS:

1. In a large mixing bowl beat butter with an electric mixer on medium to high speed for 30 seconds.

2. Add sugar, baking powder, baking soda, and salt; beat until combined.

3. Beat in the eggs, vanilla, and almond extract until combined.

4. Beat in as much of the flour as you can with the mixer. Stir in any remaining flour with a wooden spoon.

5. Stir in the anise and fennel seed, the cranberries, pistachios, and apricots (I omit the apricots, but do as you wish.)

   *The first time I made this recipe I didn't have any apricots on hand and decided to just make it without them. I love the recipe without them so much I have never been tempted to add the apricots back in. But again, if you are a lover of apricots, feel free to give them their rightful spot back in the recipe.*

6. Cover and refrigerate for 2 hours or until dough is easy to handle.

7. Preheat oven to 350 degrees Fahrenheit.

8. Divide the dough in half. Shape each half into a 12-inch long log about 1 1/2" thick.

9. Place logs 3 inches apart on a stoneware baking sheet. Flatten each log to a 1/4" thick loaf.

10. Combine the 1 egg and 1 T water. Brush egg mixture over loaves.

11. Bake in a preheated oven for 25-30 minutes or until light brown. Cool loaves on baking sheet for 1 hour or until completely cool. (When I'm baking these in the holiday months I just take my baking sheet and set it out in my back porch area to help the cooling process go more quickly.)

12. When loaves are cool, preheat oven again to 325 degrees Fahrenheit. Transfer loaves to a cutting board. Cut each loaf diagonally into 1/2" thick slices. Lay slices, cut sides down, on baking sheet.

13. Bake in the preheated oven for 5 minutes. Turn slices over; bake for another 5 minutes, or until biscotti are dry and crisp. Transfer to a wire rack; cool.

Here's where the original recipe ends but I add a little something. Melt white chocolate chips or a couple chunks of almond bark, either in microwave at 30 second intervals, or on the stovetop in a double broiler. Take a fork and drizzle the white chocolate or almond bark over one side of the biscotti. It adds just the right amount of sweetness to this crispy cookie treat.

Makes about 36 biscotti. To store: Place in layers separated by waxed paper in an airtight container; cover. Store at room temperature or freeze for up to three months.

# Reflections

_____

_____

_____

_____

_____

_____

_____

_____

_____

_____

_____

_____

_____

_____

_____

_____

_____

_____

_____

_____

_____

# Reflections

_____

_____

_____

_____

_____

_____

_____

_____

_____

_____

_____

_____

_____

_____

_____

_____

# Stories by White Lights

One of our favorite holiday traditions is one that we stumbled upon several years ago.

It was Thanksgiving weekend, and we had just finished decorating our Christmas tree. I was exhausted from all the work entailed with lugging boxes out of storage and finding enough working white lights to cover an 8 foot tree. The kids were hungry, and I didn't have enough time or energy to prepare a real meal, so I threw together a cheese and cracker plate. I pulled out a few veggies and dip and then warmed up some leftover frozen pizza rolls in the oven. We had a bottle of Welch's sparkling grape juice and, all together, it made up our dinner that night.

The Christmas lights were twinkling and cast a beautiful golden glow in our living room that none of us wanted to miss. So, instead of sitting at our dining table, I scoured the dark recesses of my cabinets and found some old holiday paper plates and napkins, and we made ourselves a little makeshift picnic right there next to the light of our tree. We huddled together on the floor around our coffee table, and Aaron started sharing favorite Christmas memories. Soon he was asking the kids to share, and before we knew it, we realized something special was happening. It was the beauty of the tree that drew us in but the sharing of our stories that kept us there. That night was like an unexpected and somewhat magical gift.

Now, almost seven years later, it is one of the traditions we most look forward to. Every year, the weekend after Thanksgiving, we chop down our tree, drag it home, decorate it and then settle in for appetizers and stories by white lights.

**Sometimes the most meaningful things happen without any preparation at all.**

This season is full of planned parties, festivities, and menus. And that's not bad. There is a lot to be said for putting thought and detail into something and planning it out ahead of time. I love to have people in my home when we've scheduled it, and I have the time

to clean my house and prepare a great menu. I love to set a beautiful table and make my guests feel special. But some of the most life-giving conversations that have taken place in my house, some of the most wonderful memories that have been made, have occurred when friends have dropped by unannounced. With no expectations and zero preparation on my part. Holy conversations have been held with crumbs on my counter and dirt on my floor.

In this busy season of "scheduled everything," don't be afraid to go rogue once in a while. Toss a schedule or two to the wind and just show up somewhere. Perhaps for someone. There is beauty in the unannounced visit. There is healing in the unexpected word of encouragement. There is grace for the moment, whether you've planned for it or not.

> *Father, teach us to make room in our schedules for You. We ask for your wisdom and guidance in our decisions. May you use us in unplanned ways to speak love and hope into the lives around us. May we experience more holy moments in the middle of our days.*

# Wonderful Counselor

When Aaron and I decided to get married, my parents did something pretty great. They got us a pre-wedding gift. It wasn't anything wrapped up in paper and bows. In fact, it was the kind of gift that caused a few tears and even a little tension between myself and my future mate. They paid for pre-marital counseling.

When you first fall in love, it's difficult to imagine ever being supremely disappointed in the other person or imagining that there might be an obstacle that you can't overcome by staring into each other's eyes. This, of course, is precisely why pre-marital counseling exists. To have another person, an outside party, ask you some hard questions and give you the tools you'll need to prepare for the challenging, and also mundane, days that life will inevitably offer you.

When I think back to the weeks that Aaron and I sat together in a counselor's office, answering difficult questions, discussing expectations, recounting the family atmospheres and parenting styles we had grown up in, I realize just how important that time and those conversations were. There were things we shared with each other early on that we probably wouldn't have offered up on our own. We made decisions, declarations really, of what was going to be most important to us as a couple and what we were going to value. We were coming together to strategically set the course for our marriage and, ultimately, for the rest of our lives.

Proverbs 11:14 says, "*Without good direction, people lose their way; the more wise counsel you follow, the better your chances.*" (MSG)

Honestly, who doesn't want to better their chances? We all do. We want our marriages, our friendships, our careers, our parenting, our faith journey, our lives, **to flourish**.

Notice this verse says, "*Without **GOOD** direction...*" (emphasis mine). We don't just need direction. We need **good** direction. After all, the world is constantly offering up advice as to how we should spend our money, time and resources. That doesn't necessarily mean it's good. We don't need direction from just anybody. We need **good direction and wise counsel**. Christian counselors, pastors, and trusted friends are all great sources to receive wise counsel from, BUT we have an even greater source to turn to. We have the Holy Spirit, our ultimate counselor. According to Isaiah chapter 9, one of God's names is **Wonderful Counselor.**

In John, chapter 14: 16-17, Jesus promises the Holy Spirit. *"And I will ask the Father and he will give you another Advocate, who will never leave you. He is the Holy Spirit who leads into all truth."* Verse 26 says, *"But when the Father sends the Advocate as my representative— that is, the Holy Spirit—he will teach you everything and will remind you of everything I have told you."* (NLT)

Jesus is talking to his disciples in this chapter, preparing them for what is to come. He knows that he will be leaving them soon and that the gift of the Holy Spirit will come. These verses show us three distinct ways that the Holy Spirit can help us. First, the Holy Spirit will lead us into all truth. Second, he will teach us. And lastly, he will remind us of everything Jesus has spoken.

Romans 8:26 also says the Holy Spirit helps our weakness. *"In the same way, the Spirit helps us in our weakness. We do not know what we ought to pray for, but the Spirit himself intercedes for us through wordless groans."* (NIV)

He is our wise counsel. He leads us, teaches us, reminds us and helps in our weakness.

Psalm 73:24 says, *"You will keep on guiding me all my life with your wisdom and counsel."* (TLB)

Let's not be people who lose their way. Instead, let's be people who purposefully determine to ask the Holy Spirit for wisdom. Today let's spend a few minutes asking for His divine wisdom in our relationships. May our marriages, families and friendships become strong and healthy as we trust God's wise counsel.

> *Father, thank you for the wise counsel that the Holy Spirit gives. Thank you that we have someone to turn to when we feel weak and need help. The leading and guiding of the Holy Spirit is a supernatural gift that we are so thankful for. May we learn to turn to You first when we are in need of wise counsel.*

wonderful

counselor

# Oh Come all ye Messy Ponytails

The lyrics kept floating through my mind, burrowing a path into my soul.

**O come all ye faithful, joyful and triumphant.**

Could that include me? I wish it did, but honestly, I feel more faithless than faithful at the moment. Joyful and triumphant? More like **depressed** and **discouraged**.

The holiday season is upon us, and often it feels more overwhelming than we anticipated. This magical time of the year that we sing about and celebrate is not exempt from heartache and pain. Whether we are experiencing something difficult or we are carrying the burden of a friend or family member, these feelings seem more pronounced as we layer them over the backdrop of holiday joy and cheer.

The absence of loved ones can make us feel acutely alone in a room full of people celebrating. The loss and rejection we've experienced throughout the year come sneaking up behind us, trying to take both our joy and our breath away.

*And now I have to be faithful, joyful and triumphant? Great, I'll add that to the list somewhere between making Christmas cookies, buying teacher gifts, and cleaning my house for company. It all just feels so exhausting!*

But maybe we don't have to have everything perfectly together **before** we come. Maybe we don't have to be faithful or joyful before we come to the feet of Jesus. Perhaps the offer is extended to the exhausted and the weary as well as the triumphant. Could it be that all He's asking of us is just to come? Exactly as we are?

Come to Jesus with your brokenness and your burnt Christmas cookies. Come to Him in your yoga pants, your old tattered college sweatshirt, your messy ponytail and day two of no shower. Come with your sink full of dirty dishes and kids screaming and clamoring

around you. Come with your grief. Come with your loss. Come with your mistakes. Come to Him wherever you are with whatever you have. Come just as you are.

**It doesn't matter how you come, just that you do.**

Come behold Him.

Come adore Him.

Come worship Him.

And when we do, we discover that our simple act of obedience, our willingness to come to Jesus, changes everything. Like an exchange system where we always come out ahead. We come to Him just as we are, tired and weary, and He gives fresh perspective and renewed strength. We bring our mistakes and our regrets and He brings His grace. We come with our striving and He provides rest.

Don't be afraid to come to Him today, just as you are. Bring your heart and let Jesus' love transform you from the inside out. Don't worry about looking or feeling a certain way before you come—He already sees it all and knows it all. Come to Him just as you are (messy ponytail and all) and you will find that He is faithful to meet you there.

*Father, I pray that today we would enter into a holy exchange system with you. We bring ourselves, and all the mess that comes with it, in exchange for more of You. More of Your love, patience, kindness, and peace. Thank you, Father, that we always come out ahead when we spend time in your presence.*

# Mighty God

The book of Isaiah is full of Mighty God descriptions, the kind that paints a picture of the majesty and grandeur of the God we serve. Isaiah recounts, again and again, the declarations God makes regarding Himself and His character.

*"You are My witnesses," declares the Lord, "And My servant whom I have chosen, that you may know and believe Me and understand that I am He. Before me there was no God formed, and there will be none after Me."* Isaiah 43:10 (AMP)

**He alone is our God, and we are His witnesses.**

We can attest to God's sovereignty and His faithfulness by our testimony, our personal story of what God has saved us from and how He has changed us. If we have accepted Jesus Christ as our Lord and Savior, we have an incredible story to tell. It is one of love and forgiveness, full of grace and mercy, new life and hope.

Stories can be an incredibly powerful tool. When it comes to new products, one of the most compelling reasons to buy something is a shared story or experience from someone you know in real life. I can know all the details about a product but usually won't be persuaded to buy it until someone close to me shares a positive review. And then, I'm all in. Often, their excitement will spread and I become a walking billboard for the product, a witness to its greatness.

**The shepherds were some of the first real witnesses to Jesus.** In a sense, they became walking advertisements for the Savior of the world. Their experience couldn't be kept to themselves because it was the most joyful news they had ever heard, **and it was for everyone**. After seeing for themselves, they told everyone they could. As word spread, people everywhere heard the good news.

Luke 2:15-18 says, "When this great army of angels had returned again to heaven, the shepherds said to each other, *"Come on! Let's go to Bethlehem! Let's see this wonderful thing that has happened, which the Lord has told us about." They ran to the village and found their way to Mary and Joseph. And there was the baby, lying in the manger. The shepherds told everyone what had happened and what the angel had said to them about this child. All who heard the shepherd's story expressed astonishment."* (TLB)

The shepherds were all in. They heard a story, followed it to the source and then shared with anyone who would listen. For those of us who have heard the Good News and traced it back to God, our job now becomes to share that news with those around us. Our lives act as a witness to the world that His story is an integral part of our own story.

We have an opportunity every day to be all in, but especially during this advent season as we reflect on the birth of Jesus. We have a story to tell of how a baby born thousands of years ago set into motion a love story that would change our lives forever. This week, let's ask God to use our words to astonish people with His love and let's live our lives in a way that will bear witness to the mighty God we serve.

> *Father, we acknowledge that You alone are God. There was no one before You, and there will be no one after You. Give us an opportunity this week to share our story with somebody who needs to hear it. We give You full access to our lives and to the stories You are still writing. Give us the words to speak, that we might be witnesses to You, our Mighty God.*

# Quit Forcing It

Forcing things rarely works.

As a mom of three I've tried my hand a time or two at forcing things to happen. Forced feedings when the kids were younger as if that one last bite of green beans I shoved into their clenched mouths would somehow push them over the edge into the category of perfect health. Forced quiet time, which usually just resulted in me going into their rooms and reminding them, over and over again, to be quiet until they would fall dead asleep five minutes before we needed to be somewhere. These days, I find myself forcing my middle child to shower, as though the shower itself is some sort of medieval torture chamber designed to inflict pain upon him. I do not understand the physical aversion he has for clean water.

I've tried forcing my kids to quit fighting, to not pick their nose in public, to brush their teeth, to do their chores, to practice their instruments, the list goes on and on. I've even tried to force fun within our family. "We **will** do this activity and it **will** be fun, understood?"

But, as many times as I've tried to use force to cause a change in my children's actions, it's rarely been successful long term. Sometimes it works temporarily, but rarely does it stick.

I love the words in Matthew 11 where Jesus asks the question, *"Are you tired? Worn out? Burned out on religion?"* (MSG) Every time I read these words I find myself answering with a resounding "Yes!" I think nearly every mom who reads those first two questions feels the same way. Yes, we're so very tired, we're worn out! But I love how Jesus sneaks that last question in there. "Are you burned out on religion?" Why is He following with this question? Because He knows that forcing things, just going through the motions without our hearts being truly connected to it, will never provide the outcome we're looking for. Just being religious will never give us the true rest and freedom our souls crave. Jesus tells us in verses 28-30, *"Come to me. Get away with me and you'll recover your life. I'll show you how to take a real rest."* Have you ever heard anything more alluring in your entire life?

The verse goes on to say, *"Walk with me and work with me—watch how I do it. Learn the unforced rhythms of grace. I won't lay anything heavy or ill-fitting on you. Keep company with me and you'll learn to live freely and lightly."* Just reading these words fills my heart with hope.

The freedom that Jesus offers us is found in the unforced rhythms of His grace. It is found in His presence when we keep company with Him. It's also something we have to learn; it's not something that comes naturally. Honestly, following rules and checking off boxes comes much more easily. We like to say to ourselves, "There, all done." while God is saying to us, "Here, just come."

> *Father, help us to quit forcing things and to start living freely and lightly in Your unforced rhythms of grace. May we not look to religion to give us rest, but may we recover our lives as we live in relationship with You. Thank you for Your promise that, as we walk with You and work with You, You will show us how that looks. Our hearts crave the real rest that only comes from You.*

## CRANBERRY SAUCE +
## CRANBERRY AVOCADO SALAD

This time of year is perfect for cooking with cranberries. Their color is divine, and the tart taste complements so many dishes. I love having a great appetizer or side salad to bring along to a party. Here are two of my favorites: one uses fresh cranberries, and the other one dried. They are both easy recipes to make and pack a flavorful punch. Enjoy!

## CRANBERRY SAUCE

*by Sue Williamson*

I got this recipe from my dear pastor's wife, Sue Williamson, when we were on staff with them in Hibbing, MN. I still have vivid memories of our first board/staff Christmas party together where she spoiled us with a plethora of delicious dishes. I can't count the number of times Becky Reini, our associate pastor's wife had us over for mouth-watering meals. My recipe collection really got a boost while living there. But, even more than all of the great food that was served, was their motivation behind it: to serve others. I am so thankful to have been able to sit under their leadership during those first years of ministry. They both hold a special place in my heart.

INGREDIENTS:

- *1/2. c. water*
- *1/2 c. sugar*
- *1/2 c. brown sugar*
- *1 bag of fresh cranberries (12 oz.)*
- *3 T. Horseradish*

- *1 T. Dijon mustard*
- *1 lb. cream cheese*
- *crackers*

39

## DIRECTIONS:

1. Boil the water and sugars together over medium heat and add fresh cranberries

2. Return to a boil. Lower heat and cook another 10 minutes, stirring occasionally.

3. Spoon into a bowl and allow it to cool to room temperature. Stir in Horseradish and Dijon mustard.

4. Cover and chill. Pour sauce over a pound of cream cheese and serve with crackers.

# CRANBERRY AVOCADO SALAD

## INGREDIENTS:

- 2 (5 oz.) bags mixed salad greens
- 2 ripe avocados
- 1 c. walnut halves, sugared and toasted *
- ¾ c. dried cranberries
- ½ c. blush wine vinaigrette (I prefer the Brianna's brand, but any will do)
- ¼ t. ground pepper

## DIRECTIONS:

Mix the salad greens, sliced avocados, sugared walnuts, dried cranberries, vinaigrette and pepper and toss until coated. Serve immediately.

*To sugar and toast walnuts: add 1/4 c. sugar to a pan with the nuts and cook over low heat until the sugar is melted.

# Reflections

_____

_____

_____

_____

_____

_____

_____

_____

_____

_____

_____

_____

_____

_____

_____

_____

_____

# Reflections

_____

_____

_____

_____

_____

_____

_____

_____

_____

_____

_____

_____

_____

_____

_____

_____

_____

_____

_____

_____

_____

# Everlasting Father

I have such fond memories of time spent with my dad while I was growing up. The two of us in his rusty, green pickup truck, heading out to my grandpa's farm to cut down a tree and bring it home to heat our log house. My favorite part was when he would signal "break time" and then proceed to pull out a thermos of hot chocolate and a candy bar to split, usually a Hershey's chocolate bar with almonds. We'd sit and enjoy our snack as well as the break from the hum of the chainsaw. Sometimes we'd chat, but usually, we just sat there in the silence, enjoying each other's company and the smell of the crisp air mixed with freshly cut wood shavings.

I am incredibly blessed to have both my parents living and in great health. Now my children get to create sweet memories of lazy days spent on my parent's dock, catching fish, and sipping sun tea in their bare feet in the same place that formed me into the woman I am today. It honestly makes me ache to think about there ever being a time when I won't have my father here to invest in my life or to teach my children how to properly clean a fish. But I know that life is precious, and his physical presence in my life is not a guarantee.

I'm so thankful that I can depend on the eternal and everlasting presence, love, and wisdom of my heavenly Father. Isaiah 40:28 says, *"Do you not know? Have you not heard? The Lord is the everlasting God, the Creator of the ends of the earth. He will not grow tired or weary, and his understanding no one can fathom."* (NIV)

Even the most amazing fathers will grow tired from time to time. Just ask my kids. They will be the first to tell you what a great dad they have but they will also let you know that Sunday afternoons equal dad's nap time. After a long weekend of running three church services, their pastor daddy is tired. He grows weary.

How comforting it is to know that we can rest our cares, our anxious thoughts, our tired hearts, in God's loving arms. We can rest in the knowledge that, regardless of

45

how our earthly father feels about us, we are seen, known, and loved by the Creator of the universe. Some of us have had amazing earthly fathers like mine, while others have suffered terribly at the hands of those who were supposed to love and protect us. But regardless of how our earthly fathers have been, we are infinitely loved by our heavenly Father. He sees us as we are, loves us regardless, and desires to have a relationship with us. And when we accept His love for us, we are held together by a love that is beyond our understanding. A love that does not grow tired or weary. An everlasting love that comes from an everlasting Father.

*Thank you, Father, that You are a perfect example of everlasting love. We come to You today, in need of that love. Take us in Your arms and speak words of comfort and hope over us today. We grow tired and weary, but You never do. Renew our strength today as we wait on You.*

Everlasting Father

# The Gift of Acceptance

Have you ever had a hard time accepting a gift?

Most people would probably say "no," but there have been a few moments in my life when I've been given something so special it made me slightly uncomfortable. Whether it's something tangible or the gift of a compliment, sometimes it's hard to be the recipient, especially if you feel undeserving.

Honestly, I find accepting help difficult most of the time. And I've talked with countless women who agree that it's just really hard to accept help from others.

I think it's because we often correlate "help" with a degree of failure on our part. Thoughts like, "I should be able to do this on my own." Or, "I hate that I can't handle this myself!" make us reluctant to accept the help that others are willing to give.

And yet Matthew 10:40-42 says this, *"We are intimately linked in this harvest work. Anyone who accepts what you do, accepts me, the One who sent you. Anyone who accepts what I do accepts my Father, who sent me.* ***Accepting a messenger of God is as good as being God's messenger. Accepting someone's help is as good as giving someone help.*** *(Emphasis mine.) This is a large work I've called you into, but don't be overwhelmed by it. It's best to start small. Give a cool cup of water to someone who is thirsty, for instance. The smallest act of giving or receiving makes you a true apprentice. You won't lose out on a thing."* (MSG)

In a world where admitting you could use help is frowned upon, we see that God's kingdom works very differently. Isn't His idea of how things should work refreshing? Here we discover that we are all intimately linked together. We discover that ***accepting*** is as important and valued as ***giving***. And we discover that the only way to accomplish all that He's called us to is by working together, learning the art and the value of both.

There is no failure tied to your acceptance of help. Rather, there is importance and value threaded into it. Jesus modeled this for us while He was here on Earth. We see many instances in Scripture of Jesus giving. He gave of his time, energy, and resources. And yet, we also see Him receiving. Jesus received the woman in Bethany who broke her expensive jar of perfume and poured it on His head. He received the hospitality that Martha offered Him and the rapt attention that Mary gave. He even received Simon's help as He carried His cross to be crucified.

If our desire is to be a disciple of Christ, then we need a shift in our thinking. We need God to transform our minds and our hearts. We need Him to reveal some of the misconceptions that we have regarding receiving help from others. We need a reminder that we are all in this together and that as we learn the holy rhythm of giving and receiving, we become more like Him.

> *Father, make us more like You this holiday season. Show us the benefit of learning to accept and receive not only from others but also from You. May we sense the value in linking arms with those around us to get the job done. It is a large work that you've called us to and we each have our own part to play. Thank you, Father, for modeling this concept for us and continue to work it out in our lives in the days ahead.*

# Prince of Peace

Living in the world we do, the idea of peace can sound like something straight out of the pages of a fairy tale. A lovely little made up word with no real-life substance to it.

We often define peace as an absence of violence, war, or strife. While that is certainly one definition, it may cause acute disappointment when we realize that we will never live in that kind of world. Recently we witnessed missiles launched at Syria after a chemical attack. We continue to see gunman all over our country take the lives of innocent people because they are blinded by hate. Humanity stooped so low this year that a gunman murdered his grandfather and posted the video to Facebook. So where does that leave us? Peace seems to be something far beyond our reach.

But what if peace is **less about the absence** of something and **more about the presence** of something? Or better yet, Someone.

Scripture tells us that God is our source of peace, Yahweh Shalom (Judges 6:24). As we continue to be in right relationship with God, one of the benefits that we receive is peace. Isaiah 26:3 says, *"You will keep in perfect and constant peace the one whose mind is steadfast (that is, committed and focused on You-both inclination and character), because he trusts and takes refuge in you."* (AMP) According to this scripture, the threat of war or evil has no impact on our peace. In fact, no outside circumstances have any bearing on the peace that is found in Christ. As we stay committed and focused on Him, He provides us with His peace that passes all understanding. Paul says in 2 Thessalonians, *"Now may the Lord of peace himself give you peace at all times and in every way."* (NIV)

This is our answer! This is how we can live in a broken and sinful world but also experience peace in the midst of it all. We keep our mind on God, we place our trust in Him, and we take refuge in Him. **The Lord of peace will give us peace at all times and in every way.** What an amazing promise.

If we believe this, then peace is available to us in any circumstance. Whether we are watching the news or reading another article online of the latest violent attack, we can have peace. At all times and in every way. Whether we are stressing out because we're late getting our kid to their holiday concert, or embarrassed that they are showing up in black dress shoes two sizes too big for them, we can have peace. At all times and in every way. Whether the demands of family and holiday parties threaten to push us to our breaking point or we find ourselves wondering if this will be our last Christmas to celebrate with a loved one, we can have peace. At all times and in every way.

May we remember that our peace isn't dependent upon our circumstances, but dependent upon our decision to keep our minds steadfast on God. We can choose peace by choosing to place our focus on Him.

> *Thank you, God, for the peace that is available to us through You. You are the Lord of peace and You give us peace at all times and in every way. We acknowledge that You alone are our source of peace and we ask today that, as we keep our minds steadfast on You, that You would cover us with Your peace that passes all understanding.*

prince

of

peace

# A Perfect Miss

My family believes strongly in cutting down a real tree for Christmas. If we had a family manifesto, our stance on this would surely be written in ink. What is Christmas without the scent of real pine wafting through your house for the entire month of December? *We are those people.* The ones that load up the entire family into the car the weekend after Thanksgiving and head off to a Christmas tree farm in search of the perfect tree. We trounce through the snow inspecting each one. Some only get a glance from us, they are too skinny, or too short, or too sparse, and our eyes quickly skip to the next candidate. Those that, upon quick inspection, meet the basic criteria, are then moved into an elimination round. When we've narrowed it down to our top two or three trees, we then move into family voting. Every person gets one vote and whichever tree receives the most votes, wins.

I admit that last year things took a turn for the worse when, after promising our daughter the year before that she could have the final say, my husband went rogue and trumped her tree choice with his veto power. It took her to the ground in tears and ruined the whole experience for all of us.

**Sometimes, in our quest for perfection, we trample down all the joy in the process.**

We didn't go into the tree selection process thinking it would end with Hannah on the ground in tears. We just wanted the most perfect Christmas tree we could find. But somehow, along the way, we experienced tunnel vision and forgot to enjoy the process.

The holidays are full of moments where we try to create perfection. We want to take the perfect family photo, have a perfectly decorated house and Christmas tree, and we want to make perfect little Christmas cookies with our perfect little kids. It's a recipe for disaster.

When we focus more on the "what" (perfect tree) than we do the "who" (our daughter) we miss out. We need to remind ourselves to look up from what we're doing and just

55

enjoy the sweet little moments along the way. The smiles and the giggles are worth way more than a perfectly frosted cookie.

*"Yet God has made everything beautiful for its own time. He has planted eternity in the human heart, but even so, people cannot see the whole scope of God's work from beginning to end."* (NLT)

When I find myself in this vortex of perfectionism, and I feel it pulling me in, I have to remind myself that there is beauty in the process. There is beauty in the perfectly imperfect mess of it all. Often, it's in the wreckage of our expectations that we find some remarkable moments.

I pray this holiday season would be one where we see the beauty in all that life offers. From the imperfect family photo to the delicious yet haphazardly decorated cookie, there is beauty to behold in all of it. I pray that we would find joy in the process, however that might look for us. I pray that we would be free from the stress and worry that can threaten to drag us under during this busy season and that our homes would resound with a gentle peace. May our quest for perfection be replaced with a sense of gratitude for what we already have.

> *Father, You make all things beautiful in Your time. We give You all of our imperfect messes and trust You with them today. We release our grasp on trying to make things perfect and open our hands, surrendering it all to You. Remind us of what is truly important this holiday season and give us a fresh perspective to see all the beauty that today holds. Thank you Father that You alone are able to give us beauty from the ashes we offer you.*

# Emmanuel : God with Us

Being present is one of the greatest gifts you can give someone.

Whether you're gasping for air as you and your friend throw your heads back in laughter, or whether they're grasping your hand in a desperate plea as tears fall down their cheeks, your presence can make all the difference.

I can still recall the many faces of friends and family who came to pay their respect at my father-in-law's funeral. So many people came from all over the state and country to give us the gift of their presence. It meant so much to us. Simply having them there was enough. I can't specifically recall any of the words spoken to me that day, but I do remember feeling incredibly loved and cared for.

**There are times when our presence speaks louder than any words ever could.**

I love that one of the names for God is Emmanuel, literally meaning "God with us." His presence in our lives brings comfort to us. Sometimes, when life gets rough and we feel like we don't understand what's going on, just knowing that He is with us is enough to keep us afloat.

Psalm 139 talks about God being everywhere. In fact, in the NSRV version, the chapter is titled: "The Inescapable God." I love that. There is no escaping Him, He is with us no matter where we go. Verses 1-12 say, *"You have searched me, Lord, and you know me. You know when I sit and when I rise; you perceive my thoughts from afar. You discern my going out and my lying down; you are familiar with all my ways. Before a word is on my tongue you, Lord, know it completely. You hem me in behind and before, and you lay your hand upon me. Such knowledge is too wonderful for me, too lofty to attain. Where can I go from your Spirit? Where can I flee from your presence? If I go up to the heavens, you are there; if I make my bed in the depths, you are there. If I rise on the wings of the dawn, if I settle on the far side of the sea, even there your hand will guide me, your right hand will hold me fast. If I say, "Surely the darkness will hide me and light become night around me," even the darkness will not be dark to you; the night will shine like the day, for darkness is as light to you."*

How amazing it is that God's presence both precedes and follows us. He is everywhere. He is God with us. This truth is not just for the advent season, but for every season of our lives. He is there with us in the difficult decisions, the struggle to make ends meet and the mistakes we make. He is there with us in the quiet and sometimes lonely days that follow this busy holiday season. He is with us on the days that feel like warm sunshine and on the days where it feels like the rain won't ever let up. He is our constant and there is nowhere we can go that He is not already there.

> *Thank you, Father that you came as our Emmanuel. We are so grateful for Your presence in our lives. With You, we can face anything. Your presence in our lives sustains us and gives us hope. Thank you for the hope that came in the form of baby Jesus so many years ago, but that is still ours today through the Father, Son and Holy Spirit.*

*Unto Us: An Advent Devotional*

# Rest + Recipe

## CHRISTMAS MORNING BREAKFAST

For as long as I can remember, every single year that our family gathered around the kitchen table on Christmas morning there were two dishes. One was what we called Christmas Morning Breakfast, and the other was a fruit cup of raspberries and sliced bananas. Over the years, things were added to the menu at times. My mom learned how to make a delectable almond puff pastry that was a very welcomed addition. But always taking center stage was our Christmas Morning Breakfast. It's a delicious blend of eggs, smoked sausage, and cheese along with a few other ingredients that we would then slather over a toasted English muffin. Yum....just thinking about it makes me hungry. It's such a great recipe that we should have made it throughout the year, but somehow, after achieving its Christmas Morning status, we never had the heart to make it any other day.

## INGREDIENTS:

- *1 dozen eggs (hard boiled)*
- *16 oz. smoked sausage*
- *1 stick butter*
- *½ c. flour*
- *1c. milk*
- *1 can cream of mushroom soup*
- *½ lb. Velveeta cheese, cubed*
- *English muffins*

## DIRECTIONS:

1. Boil the dozen eggs and after cooled, slice them with an egg slicer or with a knife.

2. Cut the sausage into ¼" to ½" chunks. Layer a 9x13" pan with a row of eggs and then a row of sausage, alternating as you go.

3. Make the sauce by combining the butter and flour first and then adding the remaining ingredients. Cook until melted and combined.

4. Pour sauce over the layers of egg and sausage. Bake at 350 degrees Fahrenheit for 30 minutes or until warm. Serve over slices of toasted English muffins.

# Reflections

_____

_____

_____

_____

_____

_____

_____

_____

_____

_____

_____

_____

_____

_____

_____

_____

_____

# Reflections

_____

_____

_____

_____

_____

_____

_____

_____

_____

_____

_____

_____

_____

_____

_____

_____

_____